1. Hilo's Rainbow Falls after a rain.

2. Ship traffic in Hilo Bay from Liliuokalani Gardens.

4. A chant to the sun.

5. Lava flows into the sea below Kilauea.

6. Lush green rainforests border complete desolation.

8. The Puu O'o Vent erupts.

9. Lava glows brightly as it flows into the sea.

10. The anthurium is an exotic flower of the Big Island.

11. The jade tree.

12. The Black Sand Beach at Punaluu.

14. Peace and tranquility inside the "Place of Refuge", or Puuhonua-O-Honaunau.

15. The sun sets over the Place of Refuge.

17. Churches of the Big Island.

18. Dormant Hualalai looms above Kona, Hawaii.

19. Kailua-Kona town and bay.

21. A scene at the Mauna Lani resort on Hawaii's Kohala coast.

22. The Hilton Waikoloa Village.

23. The Mauna Lani Resort.

25. Parker Ranch and the town of Kamuela.

26. A cowboy's view of Mauna Kea.

27. The scale of the Mookini heiau complex is revealed in this aerial view.

29. The North Kohala Coastline.

30. Waipio Valley from the roadside lookout.

31. "Boiling Pots" in Hilo town.